AMAZING FACTS
ABOUT EVERYTHING

Sandy Creek
NEW YORK

An Imprint of Sterling Publishing
387 Park Avenue South
New York, NY 10016

This 2012 custom edition published exclusively for Sandy
Creek by QEB Publishing, Inc.

ISBN: 978-1-4351-4402-6 (print format)

A CIP record for this book is available from
the Library of Congress.

For information about custom editions, special sales, and
premium and corporate purchases, please contact Sterling
Special Sales at 800-805-5489 or specialsales@
sterlingpublishing.com.

Manufactured in China
Lot #:
10 9 8 7 6 5 4 3 2 1
09/12

Picture Credits

Key: t = top, b = bottom, c = center, l = left, r = right

Alamy: 11t A.T. Willett, 16-17 Andrew McConnell, 21b Mike Goldwater, 29t WestEnd 61, 33c Peter Arnold Inc., 35t Unai Pena, 41t Blickwinkel, 47b Jack Sullivan, 48-49 Peter Arnold/Astrophoto, 67b Ace Stock, 82-83 Travelbild, 85b Picture Contact, 88-89 Travelpix, 92-93 JTB Photo Communications, 100 Planetpix

Ardea: 101 Graham Robertson, 105t Adrian Warren, 106-07 Thomas Marent

Corbis: 6 Scott Stulberg, 10-11 Jim Zuckerman, 12-13 Jim Edds, 14-15, 19c Eric Nguyen, 15b Arctic Images, 16b Michael Freeman, 17c Andrew Brown, 20-21 Chris Collins, 24-25 Carol Hughes, 25t Meijert de Haan, 25b Chris Hellier, 27c Bettmann Archives, 30c Andrew Brownbill, 31t Simela Pantzartzi, 32-33 TWPhoto, 35b Mainichi Newspaper/AFLO/ Nippon News, 36-37 Galen Rowell, 39b Mike Theiss, 40-41 Tom Bean,

41b Ralph A. Clevenger, 46-47 Hemis/Patrick Escudero, 56-57 Matthieu Paley, 60-61 Frontpage, 61b Frans Lanting, 66-67 Visuals Unlimited, 72-73 Hemis/Romain Cintract, 74-75 Theo Aloffs, 77r, 77 t National Geographic Society/John Bircham 79b Eddi Boehnke, 80-81 Latitude/ Philippe Body/Hemis, 81t, 85t, 89b Yann Arthus-Bertrand, Danny 87b Lehman, 89t Jonathan Blail, 91b Du Huaju/Xinhua Press, 93t David Frazier, 94-95 In Pictures/FritzHoffmann, 95t Gerd Ludwig, 4102-103 Theo Aliffs, 104-105 Martin Harvey, 107t Buddy Mays, 107b Joe Macdonald, 108-109 Matt Jeppson, 111t Rene Lynn, 110 Arthur Morris, 113br Frank Lukassek, 115b, 126-127 Anthony Bannister, 116-117 Juan Medina, 119b Jeffrey Rotman, 119t Reuters, 122-123 Kevin Shafer, 125b Louise Gubb, 127t Dennis Kunkel Microscopy, 131t Reuters, 137t Tony Savino

FLPA: 22-23 Matthias Brieter. 63t R. Dirscherl, 123b Mark Moffat, 129t Nigel Catlin

Getty Images: 8c Peter Charlesworth, 42-43 Shafer & Hill, 59t Stockbyte, 62-63, 63b Speleoresearch & Films/Carsten Peter, 67t Yomiuri Shimbun, 69b Lonely Planet Images/Grant Dixon, 71c G. Brad Lewis, 93cAFP

NASA: 50-51 Image Exchange, 64t, 65b Judy Rushing, 68-69, 96c 96-97, 98t, 98-99 Jet Propulsion Laboratory, 99b Image Exchange/Kennedy Space Station

NOAA: 13 c, 44 Ocean Explorer Gallery/Catalina Martinez, 44b, 55t, 55b Ship Collection

Photolibrary: Cahir Davitt, 70-71 Douglas Peebles, 77-78 Christian Heinrich, 84-85 Aflo-Foto Agency/Yoshio Tomii, 103b OSF, 123t Tim Scoones, 124-125 James Robinson

Rex Features: 49 Rex Features, 109b /Nature Picture Library 111b Sipa Press, 114-115 CDC/Phanie

Science Photo Library: 9b Daniel L. Osborne, 26-27 David Weintraub, 28-29 Stephen & Donna O'Meara, 45t P Rona/PAR/National Undersea Research program/NOAA, 51b Mark Garlick, 52-53 Chris Butler, 53t, 125t Steve Gschmeissner, 120-121 David Fleetham Visuals Unlimited inc., 130-131 Karl H, Switak, 132-133 Gustoimages, 135c Kurt G., 134-135 Louise Murray, 138-139 Jacques Jangoux, 139t Peter Menzell

Shutterstock: 7c Melanie Metz, 8-9 Wally Stemberger, 9t Sybille Yates, 12b Caoitlin Mirra, 18t photoflorenzo, 18-19 Suzanne Tucker, 30-31 Ververidis Vasilis, 37c Brian Finestone, 38-39 David Watkins, 44-45 Willyam Bradberry, 48b Molodec, 51t Kevin Carden, 54-55 Galyna Andrushko, 57c Jeremy Richards, 58-59 LaurensT, 64-65 Ffooter, 69t Oleg Kozlov, 73t Nikoai Stanov, 75b Debra James, 78-79 Angels Gate Photography, 83t Jonathan Larsen, 86-87 CQ, 90-91 Perkus, 113t Stu Porter, 115t Toa55, 117c p.studio66, 121t Teguh Turtaputra, 121b Lim Tlaw Leong, 127b David Dohnal, 129b Sebastian Kaulitzki, 133t Ryan M. Bolton, 133b Mark Tipping,

Miscellaneous: 23cTuorihilla, , 61t Photoshot/Oceans Image/Michael Patrick O'Neill, 31c Yellowstone National Park, 38b Reuters/Stringer Australia, 43b Reuters/Stringer, 87b Dinodia/Bridegman Art Library, 112-113 Photodisc, 118 Nature Picture Library/Jeff Rotman, 128-129 Nature PL/Kim Taylor, 131b Nature PL/Prima Photos, 134-135 Photoshot/ NHPA/Daniel Heuclin, 137b Laura Darby, 139 Gard Karlsen

AMAZING FACTS
ABOUT EVERYTHING

CAREY SCOTT

Sandy Creek
NEW YORK

CONTENTS

Words in **bold** are explained in the Glossary on page 140.

THUNDER AND LIGHTNING

FACT: Lightning can be an incredible six times hotter than the surface of the Sun—up to 54,000°F.

Lightning can carry over 100 million volts of electrical energy, capable of striking a deadly electric shock. It is a giant electric spark, crackling between the clouds and the ground. It can give someone a deadly electric shock.

Electric clouds

Lightning happens when a static electric charge builds up inside storm clouds. Movements inside them make **electrons**—tiny charged particles—collect at the bottom of the cloud. This eventually makes a spark jump across the gap between the ground and the cloud.

A lightning storm strikes downtown Los Angeles.

A lightning strike can be deadly.

The sound of lightning

Thunder and lightning are actually the same thing. Lightning is the spark you see, and thunder is the sound it makes. Because sound travels more slowly than light, the lightning appears some time before the clap of thunder can be heard.

ELECTRIC SKIES

FACT: Natural electricity can create other incredible light shows, too.

Lightning is not the only show in town. A glowing, floating ball of light, a mysterious blue glow, a red flash, a bright blue spark. Although these shows are not as spectacular as lightning, they are much rarer, so most people have never seen them.

Ball lightning makes a cool, but spooky sight in the sky.

Ball lightning

Ball lightning appears as an eerie, glowing, floating ball of electrical energy—as small as a tennis ball or as big as a beach ball. It floats around for a few moments, before fizzling out or exploding with a pop.

Electrical Elmo

Saint Elmo's fire can appear during a thunderstorm, at the top of something high and pointed such as a ship's mast. During a storm, **electrical charge** collects at high points until there is a big difference in charge between the object and the air around it. Then electricity leaves the object and flows into the air, making it glow.

Saint Elmo's fire strikes during a thunderstorm.

Sci-fi sky

A red sprite is an enormous red flash high in the sky, shaped like a jellyfish, with a wide ring-shaped body and trailing tentacles. A blue jet is a bright blue flash or spark that zooms upward. These strange sights have been spotted using telescopes at night and by people in planes and spacecraft.

A red sprite flashes in the sky above a blue jet.

9

TORNADO

FACT: A towering, roaring, twisting tornado can reach wind speeds of up to 320 mph.

Tornadoes can cause devastation, flattening homes and flinging cars around as they sweep across the land. Twisters form during thunderstorms when a column of air moves downward from a thundercloud. More air spirals around it, forming a cone-shaped funnel of wind.

A killer tornado tears up southern Maryland in April 2002. Two people were killed and 95 injured in the devastated town of La Plata.

Tornado alley

The world's most destructive tornadoes occur in a part of the central United States known as Tornado Alley. Cold air from Canada merges with warm, moist air from the Gulf of Mexico to create regular twisters. Every year, tornadoes destroy hundreds of houses and kill dozens of people.

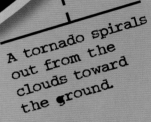
A tornado spirals out from the clouds toward the ground.

Twisting and turning

The storm forms a whirling funnel shape reaching from the clouds toward the ground. At its heart is a spinning **vortex**, which sucks dust and larger objects into it, darkening the twister. Then, it can move forward or even suddenly "hop." The biggest tornadoes can be an incredible 2½ miles across.

YIKES!

The very low air pressure inside a tornado can make glass explode, shattering windows.

HURRICANE

FACT: Hurricanes can be up to 930 miles wide, bigger than many countries.

Hurricanes form over the ocean, when warm weather makes hot, damp air rise upward. This sucks in more air, which spins around and around, building a giant spiral of swirling rain clouds. When a hurricane meets land, it brings awesome winds, huge waves, and torrential rain—causing devastation.

New Orleans flooded after Hurricane Katrina in 2005.

Ocean monsters

A hurricane begins life as a region of heated air above the warm sea. If wind speeds increase, it becomes a tropical storm. Gathering speed as it travels across the ocean, it can pick up two billion tons of water, as **vapor**, every day. The vapor forms clouds and, when the hurricane reaches land, the clouds release the water as rain.

A satellite image of Hurricane Katrina.

The eye of the hurricane

Hurricanes have an eye—an area of **low pressure** that is calm and quiet right in the middle of the storm. The clouds and winds circle around this still center. As the eye passes over it might seem that the hurricane has passed, but the storm is at its most powerful directly around the eye.

13

WINTER STORMS

FACT: In 1998, a severe ice storm in eastern Canada and upstate New York caused four million people to lose power.

In cold places, winter brings extreme weather— fierce snowstorms with howling winds that blow in every direction, and ice storms that can cut off communications and power. Ice storms can break power lines and bring down trees, making roads impassable.

Ice world

Ice storms occur when very cold rain falls in freezing temperatures. As the rain falls on icy-cold roads, houses, and trees, it freezes solid. Over time, a layer of very thick, heavy, slippery ice builds up. As well as causing skidding accidents on roads, ice can weigh down tree branches, roofs, and power lines until they snap.

Where am I?

A blizzard is a severe snowstorm in which heavy snowfall combines with swirling winds. The snow whirls around and fills the air, making it very hard to see any landmarks. Meanwhile, snowdrifts collect on the ground, making driving and walking almost impossible.

A jeep battles against a powerful blizzard in Iceland.

An ice storm stranding all flights from Logan airport in the US.

DESERT STORMS

FACT: Sandstorms can be over a mile tall and move at 60 mph.

A sandstorm this big approaching at such speed is a truly terrifying sight. It appears as a huge, moving mass of sand blowing across the land. Sandstorms can occur in all deserts, but are are most common in China, northern Africa, and the Arabian Peninsula.

A menacing sandstorm moves over the desert in Eritrea, Africa.

A haboob moves in on a livestock market in Sudan.

Haboob

Sudan suffers from a type of sandstorm called a **haboob**—a thick, fast-moving wall of sand and dust. Haboobs can affect towns and cities as well as rural areas, enveloping streets and buildings in up to 12 inches of sand.

Storm progress

As a sandstorm starts, grains of sand are blown over the ground. As they roll, bump, and bounce along, they loosen more and more grains of sand. The smaller sand particles get carried into the air, while the bigger ones tumble along at a lower level.

DANGER

THIS AREA IS LIABLE TO COLLAPSE FROM OLD MINEWORK

Sand collapse

A sandy beach or dune might not look dangerous, but seashore and desert dunes can be dangerous. Digging a cave or tunnel into a dune could make it collapse. Even digging a big hole on the beach can be dangerous. If the hole is very deep, the sides can suddenly cave in and trap anyone inside, and they would quickly run out of air.

HAILSTORMS

These pumpkins have taken a battering from a hailstorm.

FACT: Hailstones are solid balls of ice that can fall from the clouds in terrifying torrents.

Hail forms inside thunderclouds. Each hailstone starts as a tiny object, such as a speck of dust, a small seed, or even a tiny insect. As strong winds blow it around inside the cloud, it bumps into icy cold raindrops. They freeze solid around it, building up layers of ice. When the hailstone is heavy enough, it falls.

A severe hailstorm can devastate whole fields of crops, such as this corn.

Hail damage

In around 1900, farmers tried to prevent a hailstorm getting their crops by using anti-hail guns. These shot debris into the air in an effort to disperse the hail-carrying clouds. But this only had the affect of injuring people with the falling debris—the hailstorm came anyway.

Massive hailstones

Most hailstones are about the size of peas, but sometimes they can grow to 2–4 inches across. Hailstones this size can damage cars and property. The biggest hailstones on record fell on Aurora, Nebraska in 2003 and measured an incredible 7 inches across.

These hailstones are as big as golf balls. Ouch!

YIKES!

In 2002, a freak storm of egg-size hail in China's Henan province killed 22 people and injured 200.

RAINING ANIMALS!

FACT: Rainfalls of toads, fish, birds, jellyfish, and various other animals have all been reported.

These mysterious falls are very rare, but they have happened all around the world, for thousands of years. Experts think that sometimes a **waterspout**—a kind of tornado over water—sucks up sea or lake animals and carries them over land, where they fall back down. A strong wind may also pick up animals. Flocks of birds may fall like rain after flying into violent stormclouds or colliding with objects.

YIKES!

In 1869, the ripped pieces of an unidentified animal, probably a cow, fell to earth on California.

Surviving the fall

Sometimes, the animals survive the fall, suffering from nothing more than surprise and shock. At other times, animals have fallen to the ground frozen to death. This may indicate the height from which they fell—those frozen animals probably fell from a great height while the unharmed may have hit the ground soon after being picked up.

Frog and fish falls were reported in ancient Greece.

Fish cover the ground after a spooky shower.

Fishy tales

The Roman writer Pliny the Elder and the Greek historian Athenaeus both described fish falls almost 2,000 years ago. Fish fell in various parts of the United States in the 1800s, and squid is said to have hit Pennsylvania in 1841. In 2000, a huge fish fall landed on farmland in Ethiopia, Africa.

BEAUTIFUL SKIES

FACT: There is an awesome, glowing, multicolored light show that illuminates the sky, and is completely natural.

This light can be seen in the Arctic, the north of Scandinavia, Russia, Canada, or Alaska. It is called the **aurora borealis**, or northern lights. Another natural light effect looks like a faint, flickering flame hovering above the ground, and is called will-o'-the-wisp.

Solar wind

The aurora borealis happens because the sun throws out a stream of tiny particles known as the solar wind. The particles are drawn toward the North and South poles by Earth's **magnetic** field. When they crash into **molecules** in the Earth's **atmosphere**, they give out light, creating an awesome effect.

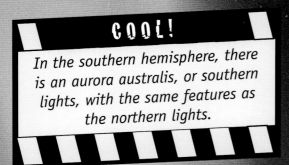
The aurora borealis illuminates the sky over a tent in North America.

A will-o'-the-wisp glows brightly in the marshes.

What is it really?

No one is 100 percent sure what causes a will-o'-the-wisp. Most scientists think it is made of gas from rotting plants, bubbling out of swamps and marshes, which may somehow light up or catch fire.

NATURAL SPIRALS

FACT: Dust devils, waterspouts, and whirlpools are all created by columns of spinning air.

A dust devil is a spinning spiral of wind that picks up dust or sand as it whirls along. A waterspout is a towering, swirling wind spiral, which sometimes occurs when a tornado forms over the ocean. A whirlpool is a spiraling body of water in a sea, lake, or river.

Dust devil

Dust devils are usually small—sometimes only as big as a person—but they can be up to 300 feet wide and as high as 1,000 feet. The strong wind and fast-flying particles in a dust devil can be dangerous.

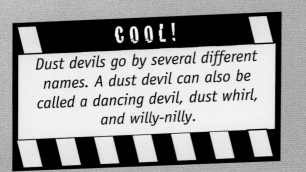

Round and round

Whirlpools usually form where fast-moving tides, or one river flowing into another, cause the water to flow in a huge spiral. Sometimes the water is sucked downward as well as going round and round.

Mokstraumen in Norway is one of the world's most powerful whirlpools.

A huge waterspout off the northern Dutch coast above the Wadden Sea.

Waterspout

When a tornado passes over a body of water, it may suck up water into its center, forming a waterspout. It may suck up fish too! Waterspouts can occur on lakes or on the ocean, usually close to the shore.

VOLCANO

FACT: There are around 1,500 active volcanoes in the world, some of which erupt continuously—spewing out hot lava (melted rock), gas, and burning ash from inside Earth.

Most volcanoes occur along the margins of Earth's **tectonic plates**, but some are found at regions called **hotspots**, such as the Hawaiian Islands and Yellowstone. Most volcanoes erupt many times, forming mountains.

Volcanic eruption

As the hot molten rock—called **magma**—inside the Earth pushes upwards, pressure increases until it breaks through the surface. Then, rock, ash, and **lava** erupt into the air, creating a volcano. The most powerful volcanoes pour clouds of ash high into the sky, blocking out the sunlight, devastating crops, and settling on buildings for miles around.

COOL!

In 1963, an undersea volcano off Iceland poured out so much lava and ash it formed a new island, 1 sq mile in area.

Pompeii

The ancient Italian city of Pompeii was flattened by the eruption of the volcano Vesuvius in 79 CE. The ash hardened around the victims' bodies, forming human-shaped cavities. In 1860, when the city was first excavated, casts were made of these cavities with plaster of Paris. The casts show people moments from death, trying to hide or escape from the eruption.

LAVA FLOW

FACT: Lava can be up to 2,200°F—five times hotter than the hottest kitchen oven.

Lava starts life inside Earth as molten rock called magma, but when it erupts into the air it becomes a gushing river of lava. Its heat is so intense that lava can set fire to plants as it flows past them, or boil water when it hits rivers or the sea.

COOL!

The volcanic rock pumice is the only rock that floats in water. It is full of holes, formed by natural hot gases.

Lava flow

Some volcanoes erupt very gently and quietly. There's no big explosion—just lava flowing down the volcano's sides. There can even be a lava flow without a volcano. Sometimes magma comes to the surface of the Earth's crust in an unexpected place, forming a new volcano.

A river of boiling lava. Such rivers are slow moving so are not usually dangerous to humans.

Ashes, gases, blocks, and bombs

As a volcano explodes, it flings out blocks of solid rock, as well as bombs—big blobs of lava that cool and harden as they fly through the air. It also releases burning hot gases and choking ash. Sometimes all of these combine in a fast-flowing river called a **pyroclastic flow**—one of the scariest types of volcanic eruption.

A volcanologist risking a roasting while collecting a lava sample.

The erupting crater of Mount Etna, an active volcano in Sicily

WILD FIRE

FACT: When fire sweeps through forests, fields, or outback, it's called a wildfire.

Some wildfires start naturally—sparked by lightning, a volcanic eruption, or dry grass and wood heating up and bursting into flames. Others are caused by people, accidentally and sometimes deliberately. Wind fans the flames and helps the fire spread. A wildfire can devour a vast area of countryside or even set a whole city ablaze.

A wildfire rages in Victoria, Australia.

Wildfire management

Also known as bushfires and forest fires, wildfires are sometimes left to burn themselves out, and the vegetation to recover naturally. But if a wildfire becomes very large, or approaches a built-up area, then firefighters are called in.

Stay or go?

When wildfires spread close to people's homes, lives can be lost. Sometimes people stay in their houses, spraying water on them to stop them from catching fire—but this doesn't always work.

Fire disaster in Chalkidiki, Greece.

Around 1.2 million acres of woodland burns in wildfires in the USA every year.

A firefighting airplane battles a firestorm on the edge of Athens, Greece in 2007.

Firestorm

A firestorm is a very intense, dangerous kind of wildfire that creates a fiery windstorm. Sometimes, a wildfire creates powerful whirlwinds and even lightning. If winds then fan the flames, the fire becomes superhot. As well as spreading the fire, firestorm winds fill the air with choking smoke.

EARTHQUAKE

FACT: The ground under our feet seems solid and secure, but it can suddenly shake, shudder, ripple, and even crack apart.

Earth's crust, is made up of several large sections, called tectonic plates. These slowly move around, squeezing and grinding against one another. Sometimes, they catch one another, and the tension builds up until the plates suddenly slip. Then, the ground jerks and trembles in an earthquake. A big one can tear cracks in the ground, causing buildings to collapse.

A collapsed freeway following the 1995 quake in Kobe, Japan.

Where they occur

Earthquakes are more frequent, and more severe, in places that lie near the edges or boundaries of tectonic plates. The country that is most prone to earthquakes is Japan. There are more than a thousand quakes there every year. In 1995 a massive quake hit the city of Kobe, causing the deaths of more than 5,000 people.

San Andreas fault

The area where two of Earth's tectonic plates meet is called a **fault line**. The San Andreas fault line extends for 750 miles through central California, and is the cause of frequent earthquakes. The most destructive hit San Francisco in 1906, killing more than 3,000 people and destroying around 80 percent of the city.

The scary destruction caused by an earthquake in California.

TSUNAMI

FACT: The Indian Ocean tsunami of 2004 was one of the worst natural disasters ever.

Waves as tall as skyscrapers hit 14 countries around the Indian Ocean, killing more than 230,000 people. Tsunamis are not just massive waves, they are walls of water usually triggered by undersea earthquakes.

A tsunami sweeps over the Pacific Coast of Japan in March 2011, creating mayhem and destruction.

A giant wave slams into a promenade in the Basque Country, Spain.

The biggest waves

In a storm, ordinary seashore waves can be 40 feet high—bigger than a house. But in 1958, a massive landslide at Lituya Bay, Alaska, caued a tsunami wave an incredible 1,720 feet high. That's taller than the Empire State Building, and the highest wave ever recorded.

Journey of a tsunami

Often, a tsunami starts as a big ripple spreading out from where it started. At first, the wave can be rather low—just a few feet high. But as the wave approaches land, it grows into a towering wall to crash onto the shore.

Destruction caused by a tsunami in Hilo, Hawaii.

Saving lives

The Pacific Tsunami Warning Center uses a siren and broadcasts to tell people when a tsunami is approaching. People can then save themselves by fleeing to evacuation sites, but their homes may still be flattened.

YIKES!

The earthquake that caused the 2004 Indian Ocean tsunami released energy equivalent to thousands of nuclear bombs.

35

AVALANCHE

FACT: As winter sports become more popular, the number of people killed in avalanches increases too.

Many things can cause avalanches—wind, sunshine melting the snow, snowmobiles or skiers dislodging it, or new snow piling up into an unstable heap. Avalanches can be deadly if the snow buries people or houses. It is heavy and hard to dig through, and people often run out of air before rescuers can reach them.

Avalanche alert!

When snow falls on mountains, it collects in large piles, or packs. After a long time, the pack collapses under the weight of the snow from later snowfalls. It all tumbles down the mountain at up to 80 mph, burying anything in its path.

An avalanche roars down Cordillera Blanca Mountain Range in Peru.

A rescue worker flies under a helicopter with an avalanche victim in a stretcher.

Avalanche rescue

Many skiers now carry an avalanche transceiver. This gadget gives out a radio signal that lets rescuers locate then if they are buried in the snow. Finding victims fast is vital—90 percent of people found within 15 minutes survive, but only 30 percent survive for more than 30 minutes.

FLOOD

FACT: In 1997-8, torrential monsoon rains caused 10 million Bangladeshis to lose their homes.

Many rivers flood the land around them every year without causing problems, because people know what to expect. But sudden, unexpected flooding can be much more serious. Floodwater can sweep away people, cars, and houses, or cause damage and spread disease by spreading mud and sewage far and wide.

The Cuyahoga River near Akron, Ohio, frequently floods its banks.

A flooded busy street in Toowomba, near Brisbane, Australia, in January 2011.

Causes of floods

In Australia, tropical storms are usually the cause of flooding. High tides threaten the low-lying cities of northern Europe. Monsoons and wet seasons cause regular flooding in the Bay of Bengal and in parts of central Africa. The southeastern USA and central America are regularly affected by river floods.

Flash floods

Flash floods occur suddenly, and are usually caused by a thunderstorm dropping a lot of heavy rain in a short time. A dam collapsing can also cause a flash flood. Many of the victims of flash flooding do not die from drowning, but from being hit by rocks, branches, and logs carried by the powerful surging water.

Hurricane Dean caused severe flash floods in August 2007 in Dominica.

39

ICE WORLD

FACT: In 1983, a research station in Antarctica recorded the coldest temperature ever -128.6°F.

Antarctica is a massive, ice-covered continent, and the world's most southerly place. At its polar opposite is a vast frozen ocean called the Arctic. In the 19th century, polar expeditions penetrated these remote icy worlds. Today, they are home to numerous scientific research stations.

Hikers climbing Mt Piz Palu, glacial landscape in Switzerland.

Glaciers

A **glacier** is a massive, slow-moving river of ice. Glaciers can have deep cracks or **crevasses** in them—sometimes as deep as the glacier itself. These are dangerous for mountaineers and explorers.

YIKES!

An iceberg caused one of the most famous disasters in history—the sinking of the Titanic in 1912.

Ice sheet

Lying over most
of Antarctica is
the biggest mass
of ice in the world.
The Antarctic ice sheet
covers an area as big as
the United States and Europe
put together. In parts, it is
more than 2.5 miles deep, and
it contains 80 percent of the
world's fresh water.

Iceberg

An **iceberg** is a
huge, floating chunk
of ice that has
broken off from a
glacier. Icebergs
form around the
Arctic and
Antarctic, where
glaciers flow
into the sea and
break up. Ice is
slightly lighter
than water. This
means that
icebergs float—
but only just.

43

HOLES IN THE EARTH

There are other blue holes, but The Great Blue Hole is the biggest and most impressive.

FACT: The Great Blue Hole, off the coast of Belize in Central America, measures over 1,000 feet across and 412 feet deep.

This awesome natural formation is a huge, deep hole in the seabed. It appears dark blue because it is so much deeper than the surrounding shallow water. Holes can open up on land too—sometimes suddenly.

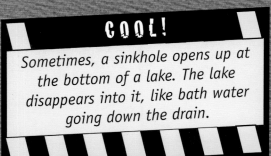
Sinkhole

A sinkhole is simply a hole in the ground caused by water wearing away underground rocks. Many sinkholes form gradually, but sometimes they can appear without warning. If this happens in a busy built-up area, it can be disastrous. When this sinkhole opened up in Guatemala City it swallowed up 12 houses and killed three people.

This sinkhole appeared in Guatemala City, Guatemala, in 2007.

From cave to hole

Experts think the Great Blue Hole formed around 10,000 years ago. The hole was then an enormous underground cave, covered by a rocky roof. When the last ice age ended and sea levels rose, the roof collapsed and seawater filled the hole. There are **stalactites** and other amazing rock formations on the hole's walls, which probably formed when it was still a dry cave.

DEAP SEA WORLD

FACT: Around 4 miles beneath the sea lies a unique deep sea world, home to bizarre creatures.

In 1977, scientists were exploring the deep sea, trying to find out why some parts of the sea contained extra-warm water. They found the answer in **hydrothermal vent sites.**

A deepsea diving vessel called Alvin was used to explore the seafloor.

Amazing discovery

They found groups of chimney-like structures—which came to be called hydrothermal vents—pouring out dark, hot water into the sea. Around the strange structures were life-forms they had never seen before.

44

Black smokers

Hydrothermal vents, or black smokers, belch out hot water containing **minerals** from the ocean floor. These minerals support a variety of bizarre life-forms, from tiny white crabs and giant mussels to worms.

Tube worms at a hydrothermal vent site.

Tube worms

These weird red-gilled white worms can grow up to 10 feet long! They have special **bacteria** in their bodies which trap chemicals from the hot vent water and convert them into food.

SCIENCE

SHAPED BY SALT

A vehicle crosses the amazingly vast Uyuni Salt Flat of Bolivia.

A salt flat—also called a salt lake—is a completely flat stretch of hard, solid salt. The Uyuni Salt Flat in Bolivia is the world's biggest salt flat, covering 4,085 sq miles. It lies 11,995 feet above sea level. The Dead Sea, located between Israel and Jordan, is actually not a sea but a huge salt lake. In fact it lies 1,300 feet below sea level.

What's a salt flat?

Salt flats form when salt and other minerals collect in a lake and the water then dries up. When it rains on Uyuni, the salt flat becomes a vast, shimmering mirror.

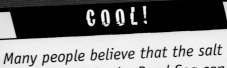

The Dead Sea's dense water makes swimmers float high up.

Lowdon lake

Most lakes have rivers running into them, and out again down to the ocean. But this is impossible at the Dead Sea, because it is much lower than the ocean. As water can't flow out, it evaporates in the hot sunshine, leaving its salt and minerals behind.

Extra salt

The Dead Sea is now more than 30 percent salt—compared to about 3 percent for normal seawater. This makes the water very dense.

47

TRICKS
OF THE SUN

FACT: A solar eclipse occurs when the moon passes directly in front of the sun.

In a total solar eclipse the moon seems to cover the sun completely and casts a dark shadow on our planet. The sun has its own tricks too—it can throw out massive explosions of energy.

An eclipse just before complete darkness.

Total and partial

A total solar eclipse happens about once every 18 months. But there are partial solar eclipses several times each year. During these, the moon covers only part of the sun.

Now the sun is completely obscured by the moon.

YIKES!

In ancient times, people believed an eclipse was a warning of a terrible event.

Solar flare

Our sun is a giant ball of superhot, burning gas. On its surface are cooler areas known as sunspots. Sometimes, near a sunspot, a powerful burst of energy bursts out. This is called a solar flare. It flings out huge amounts of radiation, such as X-rays, into space. When a solar flares heads to Earth, it may damage electronic equipment, such as satellites.

Sunspots are visible as white areas in this image of the sun.

SUPERNOVA

FACT: An exploding star, or supernova, throws out so much radiation that it can light up an entire galaxy for several months.

A supernova occurs when a large star runs out of fuel, near the end of its life span. Some stars just cool or collapse before they die, but a few get denser or heavier until they suddenly erupt.

Kepler's star

One of the most well-known supernovae was studied by German astronomer Johannes Kepler in 1604. Kepler's Star was the last supernova sighted in our galaxy, but they are often seen in other galaxies.

COOL!

The first pulsar was discovered in 1967, and was at first thought to be a message from an alien race.

When first seen in 1604, Kepler's Star was the brightest star in the sky.

Blasted to bits

A supernova explosion blasts star matter out in all directions. Sometimes, this leaves behind a big space cloud of dust and gas, known as nebula. New stars, called neutron stars, can form in a nebula when the dust starts to clump together again.

Supernova explosion, sending out shockwaves through the Universe.

A computer illustration of a pulsar, a rotating neutron star.

Pulsar

As a neutron star forms, it rotates faster and faster—sometimes many times per second. This spinning gives out beams of radiation that seem to us on Earth to flash or pulse on and off as the star spins. Because of this, it is called a pulsar.

BLACK HOLES

FACT: In space, black holes swallow up all the matter around them, such as other stars—and even light.

This is because a black hole's gravity is so strong that it sucks in anything that gets close enough. A black hole has no volume, only mass. That means it contains a huge amount of matter (stuff), so it is very heavy and has powerful gravity, but it could be tiny in area.

An artist's impression of a black hole with surrounding matter spiraling into it.

How do black holes form?

A black hole starts life as a spinning star called a pulsar. When a pulsar has a very great mass, it continues to spin and shrink and its gravity to grow until it sucks in light rays. Then it has become a black hole.

Hubble Space Telescope (HST)

We know about supernovae, pulsars, and black holes because of very powerful telescopes, such as the Hubble. Launched in 1990, the Hubble orbits Earth collecting images from distant galaxies. Incredibly, these galaxies are so far away that the light from them takes millions of years to reach us. So Hubble enables us to see events in space that happened millions of years ago.

The HST is named after the awesome American astronomer Edwin Hubble.

COOL!

In some science fiction stories, black holes can create time-travel tunnels or lead to other universes.

HIGHEST AND LOWEST

The jagged edges jutting into the air on Everest's slopes are awesomely dangerous.

FACT: **The lowest place on Earth is more than a mile deeper than Mount Everest is high.**

The world's highest mountain is 29,035 ft above sea level, and is a massive, snow- and ice-topped chunk of rock in the Himalayas, a huge mountain range in Asia. The lowest point on Earth lies 36,000 feet below the sea's surface, in the Pacific Ocean.

Conquering everest

In 1953, Sir Edmund Hilary and Tenzing Norgay became the first to reach the top of Everest and make it back home. Since then, more than 3,000 people have conquered the mountain, including a 73-year-old woman.

COOL!

Nepalese mountaineer Apa Sherpa has successfully climbed Everest an incredible 21 times.

Challenger deep

The Mariana Trench is the deepest place in the world's oceans, and Challenger Deep is the lowest point of the trench. Humans first explored the trench in 1960. Since then, several unmanned vessels have made further expeditions.

Guam

Challenger Deep

Philippines

Mariana Trench

Indonesia

The Mariana Trench lies deep in the Pacific Ocean.

Going down

In 1960, explorers Jacques Piccard and Don Walsh reached the bottom of the Mariana Trench in a diving vessel called the *Trieste*. The vessel had a very strong passenger chamber to keep the divers safe from the extreme water pressure in the deep ocean.

Piccard and Walsh in the Trieste

DRIEST AND WETTEST!

FACT: Lake Baikal in Siberia contains around 20 percent of the world's fresh water, while rainwater has never reached parts of the Atacama desert, in Chile.

Lake Baikal is the deepest lake in the world—5,315 feet—and it contains more water than any other lake. It has a rich and diverse wildlife. Animals and plants cannot survive in the dry, barren landscape of the Atacama desert.

Every winter Lake Baikal freezes over and people can ride horses over it safely.

Baikal Seals bathing in the sun.

Weird wildlife

Living in Lake Baikal are more than 1,000 species of wildlife that are not found anywhere else in the world. One of these is the Baikal seal, or nerpa. The nerpa feeds on a strange, transparent fish, called the golomyanka, which is also found only at Lake Baikal.

Why so dry?

The Atacama has mountains on both sides of it—the Andes on one side, and the Chilean coastal range on the other. When rain clouds come along, they rise up the mountains, cool, condense, and drop their rain before reaching the top. So clouds rarely reach the Atacama, lying in the middle.

Rock formations in the Atacama Desert.

MASSIVE WATERFALLS

FACT: Angel Falls, Venezuela, is the world's tallest waterfall, but Iguaçu Falls in South America is the biggest.

While Angel Falls is awesomely high, delicate, and beautiful, Iguaçu Falls is awesomely wide and loud. It has the most water flowing over it, and you can hear its thundering, watery roar from many miles away.

The Iguaçu Falls are on the border between Brazil and Argentina.

Huge horseshoe

Like many big waterfalls, Iguaçu flows over a giant horseshoe-shaped cliff, with the water splitting into many different minifalls, or cascades. The whole of the falls covers about 1½ miles, and the biggest single cataract, or large waterfall, called the Devil's Throat, is 492 feet wide.

About 62,000 cubic feet of water gushes over Angel Falls every second.

Cliff top

Angel Falls flows over an amazingly tall cliff on one side of a tepui, or table-top mountain—a typical feature of the Venezuelan landscape. From the top, the water drops straight down in a shimmering, misty column. In total, including some additional rocky falls at the bottom, the waterfall is 3,212 feet high—taller than the world's highest skyscraper.

COOL!

Angel Falls is named after pilot James Angel, who flew around the Falls in 1935 and first reported them to the outside world.

59

AWESOME RIVERS

FACT: Contrary to popular belief, not all rivers lead to the sea.

The Okavango River in Africa is a very big river, but it never reaches the sea. The Amazon River in South America is the largest river in the world and, like most other rivers, it does flow into the sea. Although it is not as long as the Nile River in Africa, it is far wider.

A stunning view of the curving Amazon River and the forest around it.

Water world

Where it flows into the Atlantic Ocean, the two banks of the Amazon River are 120 miles apart. A speedboat traveling across the river at 60 mph would take two hours to reach the other side! The river stretches more than 4,000 miles, from deep in the Amazon Rain Forest all the way to the coast.

COOL!

The Amazon River is mainly surrounded by rain forest, so there are few roads around and not a single bridge across it!

A variety of wildlife can be seen in the Amazon River, such as this bull shark.

African elephants wade through a swamp in the Okavango Delta.

Disappearing water

The Okavango River ends by flowing into a huge delta in the midle of the Kalahari Desert. There, some of the water evaporates into the hot air and the rest is sucked up by plants and drunk by animals. Every year from May to October, the river floods and brings extra water to the delta, creating a wet season.

INCREDIBLE CAVES

FACT: Mammoth Cave, in the state of Kentucky, has the longest cave tunnel system in the world.

It has 360 miles of linked passageways, filled with amazing rock formations. Malaysia is home to the world's biggest natural cave chamber, Sarawak Chamber. And in Mexico is the unearthly, awesome Cave of Crystals.

Cavers in the massive Mammoth Cave.

Underground life

Parts of Mammoth Cave have underground rivers and pools. In them live several species of troglobites—animals that have adapted to live without sunlight. These shrimp- or crab-like creatures are colourless and eyeless.

COOL!

A part of New Zealand's Waitomo Cave system is lit by thousands of glow-worms dangling from the ceiling.

Mind-bogglingly big

The Sarawak Chamber measures roughly 2,300 feet long, 1,300 feet across, and 230 feet high. Its floor is steep, bumpy, and covered in rock formations and boulders. It is like a huge, dark, underground cathedral or stadium.

Deer Cave, which is in the Mulu Caves close to Sarawak Chamber. The chamber is too dark to photograph.

Giant crystals

The Cave of Crystals is 1,000 feet below ground. The massive, geometic crystals have been formed by the mineral gypsum.

Explorers climb on the giant crystals in the Cave of Crystals.

SUPERVOLCANO

FACT: One of the bigest volcanoes in the world is not a peaked mountain, but a wide, flat, bowl-shaped feature called a caldera.

The Yellowstone Caldera in Utah is a supervolcano—a volcano so enormous and powerful that when it erupts it blasts away a massive crater in Earth. Yellowstone's last eruption was 630,000 years ago, when it left a crater 28 miles across and 47 miles long.

Satellite image of the caldera.

West Thumb Geyser Basin, in Yellowstone National Park.

YIKES!

Yellowstone could be due for another eruption. It could cover most of the USA in dust, and darken the world's sky for years.

Eruption in waiting

Yellowstone has hot springs, squirting geysers, and fumaroles, where hot gases escape from the ground. Just under the surface is a vast chamber of magma and gas waiting to erupt.

Giant fountain

Old Faithful Geyser is one of the most famous volcanic features at Yellowstone. It shoots out a jet of scalding hot water 170 feet into the air about once every 90 minutes. The water is heated by magma under the ground and made to erupt by pressure building up there.

Boiling hot water shoots out from Old Faithful.

GIANT SEA CREATURES

FACT: The blue whale is the biggest animal that has ever existed on Planet Earth—more massive than even the dinosaurs.

The blue whale's heart is the size of a small car, and some of its blood vessels are so wide, you could fit inside them! Although they are giants, blue whales are not dangerous, and are beautiful and graceful. Encountering a giant jellyfish in the ocean would be much more alarming. The Nomura's jellyfish is not only wider than a man is tall, it also looks like nothing on Earth!

COOL!

Blue whales sing to find a mate, and can hear one another's songs from hundreds of miles away.

Big and beautiful

A blue whale can grow to almost 100 feet long—about as long as four classrooms in a row—and weigh an incredible 200 tons. Blue whales are a massive, long, solid cylinder shape. They don't eat large animals, but cruise through the oceans with their mouths open to scoop up small fish and tiny shrimps.

Frilly, slimy, and stringy

With their jellylike, dome-shaped bodies and flappy tentacles, many people find jellyfish strange and disgusting to look at. Luckily, they don't feed on humans, but Nomura's jellyfish can be a danger to fishermen. In 2009, they caused a **trawler** to capsize off the coast of Japan.

A blue whale's head is about one quarter of its body length, making it one of the biggest heads on Earth.

Two Blue Whales gulp feeding at the surface of the water.

ROCKY HEIGHTS

FACT: The world's cliffs were formed millions of years ago, by glaciers flowing from the mountains to the sea, and creating deep channels in the rock.

Two tourists lie down to view the sheer drop below.

Today, many of these rocky heights are popular tourist attractions. But they can be pretty scary! Despite the many thousands of tourists that flock to Norway's Pulpit Rock every year, there is no safety rail around the cliff.

YIKES!

If you dropped a pebble off the top of Mount Thor, it would take just under 16 seconds to hit the bottom.

Cliffs of Moher

These amazing cliffs are on the west coast of Ireland, where it meets the Atlantic Ocean. They rise to more than 680 feet high, as tall as a skyscraper, and stretch for nearly 5 miles along the coast. They are also unusually **vertical**, so in many places it's a sheer drop to the rocks below.

Pulpit Rock

For people who suffer from **acrophobia**—or fear of heights—just looking at this photo of Pulpit Rock (also called Preikestolen) is probably terrifying! This awesome natural rock formation stands about 2,000 feet above Lysefjord, one of Norway's long, deep fjords, or sea inlets.

People enjoying the stunning view from Pulpit Rock.

Mount Thor and the frozen Weasel River.

Mount Thor

Mount Thor, on Baffin Island in the north of Canada, has the world's biggest vertical drop. Its overhanging cliff has a sheer 4,100-foot drop. The mountain itself is 5,495 feet above sea level, and is made of a hard rock called granite. Mount Thor was first climbed in 1953.

HAWAIIAN SITES

FACT: All the islands of Hawaii were formed by volcanic eruptions under the sea.

These enomous sea cliffs were originally part of a tall volcano. When part of the volcano fell away into the sea, the steep cliffs were left behind. Some of the Hawaiin island volcanoes are still erupting today. Kilauea is the world's most active volcano, releasing its lava in a constant, gentle flow.

You can't reach Kalaupapa by car, only by boat, plane, mule, or on foot.

Kalaupapa cliffs

On the island of Molokai in Hawaii, towering over the tiny village of Kalaupapa, are some of the world's most enormous sea cliffs. Covered with tropical plants, the giant, otherworldly green cliffs plunge just over 3,280 feet down to the sea.

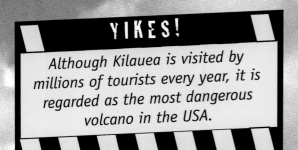
Red hot lava flows from Kilauea Volcano, Hawaii.

Kilauea

The lava that flows from Kilauea is runny and spreads out quickly, making the volcano wide and smooth. This shape has the name of shield volcano. Kilauea has several openings, or vents, where lava escapes. One of the vents, called Pu'u O'o, has been erupting continuously since 1983.

HA LONG BAY

FACT: One of the world's top tourist attractions and a UNESCO World Heritage site, this awesome limestone bay in Vietnam has to be one of the most magical places on Earth.

The calm, mirrorlike waters of Ha Long Bay are dotted with more than 1,600 rocky mini-islands, pillars, and towers. Some are covered with lush greenery and are home to all kinds of tropical wildlife, such as monkeys, lizards, and even antelopes. Around 1,500 people live there too—on floating homes.

The name Ha Long Bay means "bay of the descending dragon."

Limestone lumps

Ha Long Bay's islands have taken millions of years to form from limestone that has been shifted, shoved, worn, and dissolved by water and the movements of earth. Some of the towers are up to 656 feet high, as tall as skyscrapers. Others are hollow lumps with huge, dark caves inside.

Many people take boats to the islands to explore.

COOL!

According to legend, Ha Long Bay was formed when dragons spat out jewels, which turned into rocky islands.

GREAT BARRIER REEF

FACT: This massive coral reef is one of the world's most diverse ecosystems, and is one of the seven natural wonders of the world.

The Great Barrier Reef is the world's biggest coral reef. It is HUGE. The Reef stretches for more than 1,250 miles along the north-east coast of Australia, forming a chain of coral islands and underwater platforms that can be seen from space.

An aerial photograph of the Great Barrier Reef.

Underwater wonderland

While some coral reefs become islands, others are still underwater, where they provide a habitat, or home, for all kinds of sea creatures. Divers may see turtles, octopuses, sea snakes, jellyfish, dolphins, and more than 1,000 species of fish, including more than 100 types of sharks and rays.

Coral structure

Coral is a kind of skeleton, made by tiny sea creatures called coral **polyps**, which are a bit like sea anemones. Each polyp builds a skeleton around itself using sea minerals. Each generation builds more coral on top of the old coral, and gradually a big structure, or reef, builds up. There are many different species of coral polyps.

A scuba diver observes some of the coral of the Great Barrier Reef.

THE GRAND CANYON

The Grand Canyon, with the Colorado River flowing through it.

FACT: The Grand Canyon in Arizona is one of the biggest, most breathtaking rock formations anywhere in the world.

The Grand Canyon is a gorge—a steep-sided river valley. The high cliffs on either side are striped in stunning shades of color, made up of bands of rock of different types and ages. Unlike many other gorges, the Grand Canyon is very wide, varying from 600 feet to 19 miles across. At its deepest, it is almost 1.25 miles deep and it reaches nearly 280 miles in length.

How did it form?

Gorges form when a river cuts through rock as it flows. Over millions of years, the Colorado River has carved its way down through the landscape to create the massive Canyon. The river still flows along the bottom today.

Built to thrill

In 2007, a skywalk was built so that visitors can get a really awesome view of the Canyon. The U-shaped walkway extends 70 feet over the edge of a sheer cliff, and has a glass floor. It is made of six layers of superstrength glass, each tough enough to stop a bullet!

There can be as many as 120 people on the skywalk at any one time.

Visitors must wear special slippers when walking on the glass.

YIKES!

Every year, hikers have to be airlifted from the Canyon by the Park Service, after becoming dehydrated and exhausted.

NAMIB DESERT

The stunning red dunes of Sossusvlei, in the Namib desert.

FACT: The Namib in Africa is thought to be the oldest desert on the planet—it has been dry as a bone for around 55 million years.

It is also one of the world's most strange and beautiful places, with its soaring **dunes** and the spooky Skeleton Coast. The pointy, red-brown dunes form when the sand shifts and rolls down one side of the dune, leaving a razorlike ridge along the top.

YIKES!

The Skeleton Coast gets its name from the whale and seal skeletons that covered its shore in the time of the whaling industry.

Weird wildlife

Some of the creatures that live here have developed curious habits to cope with the heat and lack of water. The sidewinder snake skips sideways across the ground to keep as much of its body as possible off the hot sand. The Namib desert beetle lets water droplets from fog collect on its body, then lifts its bottom to tip the water into its mouth.

The Skeleton Coast

Sailors used to call this strip of deadly, foggy desert coastline The Gates of Hell. Hundreds of ships have been wrecked along the Skeleton Coast, after being lost in the fog and run aground. Over time, sand is blown out to sea and makes more land, so wrecks can be found far from the shore.

A spooky shipwreck lies forgotten on the coast in the Namib desert.

THE PYRAMIDS

FACT: The Great Pyramid of Giza is the only one of the Seven Wonders of the Ancient World still standing today.

COOL!

In ancient times, the pyramids of Giza were covered with polished limestone pieces that made the surface smooth and white.

The Great Pyramid is the biggest of three huge pyramids built by the ancient Egyptians at Giza, near the city of Cairo, in Egypt. The pyramids were built as grand tombs for the leaders called pharoahs. In Mexico, the ancient Mayan people built pyramids, too, but these were designed as temples. The most awesome site of all is at the Mayan ruins of Chichén Itzá.

Religious ruins

Chichén Itzá is a complex of several pyramids, buildings, carvings, and statues. It was an important center of worship from about the year 900 to 1100. The biggest building at the site is known as El Castillo (the Castle), which is actually a pyramid with steps and a temple on top. It was built around 1,000 years ago and dedicated to Kukulcán, a feathered snake god.

As well as temples, the Mayan pyramids were used for observing the night skies and charting the movements of the stars and planets.

How did they build them?

The Egyptian pyramids were constructed more than 4,500 years ago, with no cranes, bulldozers, or power tools. Experts think thousands of men, perhaps slaves, must have worked together to cut, shape, and haul the blocks of stone and fit them together into a perfect pyramid.

GIANT STATUES

FACT:
No one knows for sure how or why the awesome Easter Island statues were constructed.

In 1722, Dutch explorer Jacob Roggeveen landed at a tiny volcanic island in the Pacific Ocean. As it was Easter Day, he named the island Easter Island. The island was dotted with enormous statues of humans—up to 72 feet tall, known as **moai**. Experts think they may have been made as a form of ancestor worship. The giant statues at Mount Rushmore in South Dakota are a form of ancestor worship too.

Mount Rushmore

The faces of four great presidents from history—George Washington, Thomas Jefferson, Theodore Roosevelt, and Abraham Lincoln—are carved into the grey granite cliffs of South Dakota. Nearly 400 workers assisted the sculptor, Gutzon Borglum, between 1927 and 1941.

Each face is a gigantic 60 feet high.

The famous Easter Island Heads.

Humongous heads

These awesome statues are often called the Easter Island Heads. They are whole body statues, but their heads are very large, and often the lower part of each statue was buried. Over the years, most of the statues were damamged, but many have now been restored.

SEEN FROM THE AIR

FACT: The Nazca Lines—hundreds of pictures and patterns cut into the ground—are so vast that they only make sense when seen from the sky.

The Nazca Lines are on a high, flat stretch of the Peruvian Desert in South America, close to the town of Nazca. A luxury housing development in modern-day Dubai is awesome when seen from the air, too.

Some of the pictures are hundreds of feet across. This one is of a monkey.

Long-lasting lines

Experts think the Lines were made between 1,500 and 2,000 years ago. Early Nazca people created them by lifting a layer of red stones on the surface of the desert to reveal the whiter rock underneath. The patterns have survived because there is little rain or wind in the desert to disturb them.

Picture gallery

The patterns include very long, straight lines, spirals, triangles and other shapes, and animals. The lines can be several miles long. Experts think the Nazca people might have made them for their gods to look at, or to mark where water could be found.

This one depicts a spider. There are also images of birds, fish, llamas and human figures.

Palm island

For centuries, humans have created new land by filling in coastal areas with rocks and sand. In Dubai, designers realized that artificial islands in the shape of palm trees would create many miles of beach for waterfront houses.

Palm Jumeirah maximizes land area and looks amazing from above.

COOL!

Some people have suggested that the Nazca people must have been able to make hot-air balloons so that they could see the Lines' patterns.

AMAZING TOMBS

The Taj Mahal is in Agra, north India. It attracts thousands of visitors every day.

FACT: More than 20,000 workers and 1,000 elephants helped to build the Taj Mahal—a tomb for the wife of the Indian emperor.

When Mumtaz Mahal died in 1631, her husband, Shah Jahan, commissioned a beautiful tomb in her memory. The Taj Mahal is made from white marble, inlaid with 28 different precious and semiprecious stones. The tomb of Ancient Chinese emperor Shi Huangdi had a pyramid, palaces, towers, and an army of more than 8,000 soldiers to guard him and help him rule his kingdom in the afterlife.

Mourning for Mumtaz

No expense was spared in the building of the tomb. Materials came from all over Asia, and the top designers, sculptors, mosaic artists, and **calligraphers** formed the creative team. Mumtaz Mahal was buried there once the building was complete, and Shah Jahan joined her when he died in 1666.

COOL!

The Terracotta Army was hidden for more than 2,000 years, until it was discovered by farmers digging a well in 1974.

Reports say that when Mumtaz died, Shah Jahan's grief was so great that his black hair turned white.

The army includes soldiers of different ranks, as well as horses and chariots.

Pottery warriors

The soldiers from Shi Huandi's tomb are made of terra-cotta, a kind of red clay. They are life-size or a bit bigger, and each one has his own facial features. The army lay hidden from the emperor's death in 207 BCE until its discovery in 1974.

CATACOMBS

FACT: Underground tunnels dug by humans can be hiding places, scenes for religious ceremonies, or places for burying the dead.

In Paris, France and in Palermo, Italy, **catacombs** were used to store dead bodies. This happened because cemeteries became overcrowded when thousands of people died from plagues of infectious diseases.

Home for bones!

Under Paris lies a set of catacombs where human skeletons are stored. In the past, bodies were buried in big pits and when the flesh rotted away, the skeletons were collected. Where could the bones go? In the late 1700s, officials decided some old, empty stone mines in the south of the city would make the perfect underground cemetary.

Bones are stacked up all around the tunnels and rooms of the catacombs.

Mummified monk

The catacombs at Palermo contain **mummies**— preserved bodies with skin, flesh, and hair. In 1599, a monk was buried in the vault under a church. Weirdly, the monk's body had not rotted away. When people heard about this, many wanted to be buried there. The catacomb burials carried on until 1920, and now there are thousands of mummies there.

Uncannily lifelike mummies in the Palermo catacombs.

What makes a mummy?

It is not magic that makes the Palermo catacombs good at preserving bodies. It is the presence in the soil of a rock called tufa that soaks up moisture. In a very dry atmosphere, things don't rot easily, so this helps keep the mummies fresh.

One of the mummified bodies in the catacombs at Palermo.

MIRACLES OF CHINA

FACT: Entire cities were flooded to make the 370 mile-long reservoir behind Three Gorges Dam.

The Three Gorges Dam is the biggest electricity-generating power station on the planet, and has one of the world's biggest dam walls. Stretching across northern China for around 4,470 miles is the Great Wall, built from stone, brick, and soil, to protect the Chinese Empire from invaders.

Watchtower on the Great Wall.

Keep out!

People began building walls in this area 2,600 years ago. In 214 BCE, Emperor Shi Huangdi had more walls built and connected others to keep out invaders. Most of these walls have worn away. The wall as it is today was mostly built in the 1400s and 1500s to keep out Mongolian invaders.

Floodwater is diverted and controlled by the Three Gorges Dam.

Flood control

As well as generating a massive amount of electricity, the dam controls the flow of the Yangtze River, preventing it from flooding. In the past, tens of thousands of people have died when the Yangtze River burst its banks.

AWESOME BRIDGES

FACT: The first suspension bridges were built in the high mountains of the Himalayas.

Suspension bridges have the longest span of any bridges. Most have two supporting towers and cables overhead to support the bridge's main span. The Akashi-Kaikyo suspension bridge in Japan has a main span measuring 6,532 feet long, to let in the wide ships that travel the Akasi Strait.

The Akashi Kaikyo Bridge is 1.5 times longer than the Golden Gate Bridge.

COOL!

Since 1998, the Akashi-Kaikyo Bridge has held the title of the

Long and low

The longest bridges of all are **causeways**— low, simple, roadlike bridges that rest on supports standing on the sea or riverbed. Lake Pontchartrain Causeway stretches a massive 24 miles.

This awesome bridge is so long that it isn't possible to see dry land when you're standing at the halfway point.

The slight curve of the Millau Viaduct gives drivers a thrilling view.

The high road

The Millau Viaduct in France is the world's highest bridge. It is pretty long too, at 1½ miles, but what makes it so awesome is the way it towers above the landscape.

AMAZING TRAIN JOURNEYS

FACT: The Trans-Siberian Railway is 5,778 miles long—the world's longest railway.

The Trans-Siberian Railway takes about a week to complete its trip and crosses seven **time zones** in the process. But a Trans-Siberian train won't zoom along at hundreds of miles an hour. The world's speediest train trip takes place in China, on board the Shanghai Maglev.

The route

The Trans-Siberian Railway stretches right across Russia from Moscow, the capital, to Vladivostok, on Russia's east coast near Japan. It gets its name because it crosses the area of northern Russia called Siberia, but it also covers most of the width of Asia.

A train traveling past Baikal Lake in Siberia on the Trans-Siberian Railway.

Floating on air

This superfast train links the suburbs of Shanghai to its airport, covering a distance of 19 miles. Its top speed on the journey is around 267 mph. Maglev trains use powerful **electromagnets** to make the train hover just above the track. The train can go faster because there's no friction between the track and the train.

The Shanghai Maglev train zooms away from the city's airport.

INTERNATIONAL SPACE STATION

FACT: **Floating in orbit above Earth's surface is a satellite of pressurized living modules, laboratories, and work stations, where astronauts live.**

The International Space Station (ISS) is a permanent space base where astronauts study space science, and try to find out more about what life in space does to our bodies. Astronauts live there for three to six months at a time.

The International Space Station on its orbit around Earth.

Building project

As well as performing their scientific work, the astronauts who go to the ISS build more parts on it. Building began in 1998, and astronauts have been living there since 2000. Today, the station includes living quarters, science labs, and storage and service decks. It also has docking bays and an air lock so that visiting spacecraft can link to it, and astronauts can **spacewalk** outside.

Life in space

The astronauts have to live with very low gravity where things float around. Food and drinks are eaten from closed bags. The toilets have powerful suction to pull everything away. The crew sleep in sleeping bags that are tied to the walls.

Astronauts on a spacewalk, working on the International Space Station.

COOL!

The ISS is the ninth space station to be inhabited. The first, Salyut, was launched in 1971.

SPACE PROBES

FACT: A space probe called *Voyager 1* has been journeying through space since 1977.

This little **space probe** has traveled farther away from our planet than any other human-made object. It was sent to explore the **solar system** and take messages about Earth to whoever, or whatever, might one day find it.

An artist's impression of the Voyager spacecraft.

Solar system mission

At frst, *Voyager 1*'s task was to explore the planets with its onboard cameras and measuring equipment and send data back to Earth using radio signals. It took stunning pictures of Saturn and Jupiter and some of their moons. Now it has left the solar system and is moving through **interstellar space.**

COOL!
The Helios probes stopped working about 10 years after they were launched, but they still whizz around the sun every 90 days.

Attention aliens!

Both *Voyager 1* and its sister probe, *Voyager 2* (which has not traveled quite as far), carry a "Golden Record." These records contain information about Earth that could one day be discovered by intelligent life elsewhere in the universe. They include recordings of animal noises, human languages, music, pictures of Earth and humans, and scientific data.

This gold-plated aluminum cover protects the Golden Record.

A prototype of the Helios spacecraft in 1974.

The fastest machine

As *Helios 2* whizzed close to the sun, it reached a maximum speed of 157,078 mph. That's 43 miles, every single second! The Helios probes were so fast because they were in elliptical, or oval, orbit around the sun. In **ellipical orbit** objects are pulled by gravity to move faster and faster.

ANIMAL MAGIC

FACT: Every fall, monarch butterflies fly thousands of miles from Canada to Mexico.

The annual **migrations** of monarch butterflies are incredible. Not only do they travel a vast distance—they also know exactly where to go, even though they have never been there before! In their life cycle, emperor penguins have to trek for weeks, go without food, and risk freezing to death.

Hundreds of monarch butterflies on a tree trunk in Mexico.

Migrating monarchs

Most monarch butterflies live for around two months, and stay at home. But those born in the fall are different. These fly south to a warmer place. When spring comes, they mate. Then they fly back north to lay their eggs. These migrating monarchs live for around seven months.

Male emperor penguins gather together and keep the eggs safe.

Off we go!

Emperor penguins live around the coast of Antarctica—but to breed, they have to waddle 30–75 miles inland for safety. Each female lays one egg. The mom leaves the dad to keep the egg warm, by balancing it on his feet and covering it with his stomach, while she trudges back to the sea for food. She returns with some fish two months later as the egg is hatching!

REAL-LIFE DRAGONS

FACT: **Dragons don't really exist, but there are some animals that come pretty close to those fairy-tale monsters!**

The Komodo dragon is the biggest lizard in the world, growing up to 10 feet long. They have a powerful bite that injects their prey with lethal disease bacteria. The bacteria can cause death in about two days. The dragon then comes back to feast on the dead animal. North America's own horned lizard has a distinctly dragon-like habit. But instead of spurting fire, out comes blood!

Komodo dragons live on only a few islands in Indonesia, where tourists often go to view them.

YIKES!

Komodo dragons have been known to dig up human graves and eat the decaying bodies inside.

Greedy guzzler

Komodo dragons hunt large animals such as deer, and they also feed on **carrion**, or dead meat. Like snakes, they stick out their tongues to detect scents in the air and can sniff out a rotting carcass from over 5 miles away. When they find their prey, such as a dead or dying goat or pig, they guzzle it in big chunks or even swallow it whole.

Blood squirter

The horned lizard can shoot its own blood a distance of up to 3 feet away to frighten an attacker. How? The blood flow from its head to its body is cut off, so that the blood collects and pressure builds up. When the pressure is strong enough, weak blood vessels right next to the lizard's eyes burst open, and the blood spurts out.

Splat! Blood squirts from a horned lizard's eye.

REAL-LIFE VAMPIRES

FACT: There are three types of vampire bats and one of them will suck the blood of humans.

This is the common vampire bat, found in Central and South America. Vampire bats feed on blood, usually from **livestock**, and nothing else, and they need to feed every night. Like all bats, vampire bats can fly, but they like to sneak up on their victims quietly. So they walk by folding up their wings and using them as feet.

Sneaky biter

Once a vampire bat gets close and personal with its victim, it cuts into the skin with its sharp fangs. A vampire bat's saliva contains a substance to stop the blood clotting. As the blood flows out, the bat slurps it up!

The vampire bat uses its sharp front teeth to make a small, painless cut in the skin.

COOL!

A bite from a vampire bat won't harm you much—unless the bat is carrying the deadly disease **rabies**.

Big meal

A vampire bat typically takes in around half its own bodyweight in blood at one feed. It becomes so full of blood that it is too heavy to fly. So it waits a while, digests its dinner, then makes itself lighter by having a big pee before taking flight again.

A vampire bat licks up a flow of blood from its victim, in this case a chicken.

ARACHNOPHOBIA!

FACT: An irrational fear of spiders, called arachnophopbia, is experienced by more people than any other phobia.

For someone with a fear of spiders, the tarantula is probably the most horrible species. This beast is the biggest, fattest, hairiest spider in the world! A tarantula might look terrifying, but the tiny black widow spider is far more dangerous.

Tarantula's bite

For a human, a tarantula's bite is about as bad as a bee sting. But for smaller creatures, such as insects, the tarantula's bite is deadly. Its sharp fangs inject a poison that **liquifies** the victim's insides. Then it sucks them up!

YIKES!

In the town of Skuon, Cambodia, fried tarantulas are a popular snack. People breed the spiders in holes in the ground, for the dish.

Black widow spider

These spiders are found in warm countries around the world. They have very poisonous **venom**, but as they are only about half an inch long, they cannot inject much at once. Nevertheless, a bite from a black widow can be fatal for babies and the eldery. For others, it causes muscle cramps and vomiting.

Most species of black widows are black. Females have hourglass-shaped markings or spots.

The male Sydney funnel-web spider is about 1½ inches long, not including its legs.

Funnel-web spider

This Australian beast is one of the most poisonous spiders in the world. There are several species, the most dangerous being the Sydney funnel-web, and the male is much more deadly than the female. It likes water, and sometimes falls into swimming pools!

SCARY SNAKES

FACT: **Snakes live on all the world's continents except Antarctica, and in the Pacific and Indian Oceans.**

Many species are venomous, and some of them produce venom that can injure or even kill humans. Others, such as rattlesnakes, overcome their victims by constriction—strangling with their powerful bodies.

Rattlesnakes

There are about 50 different types of rattlesnakes in North, Central, and South America. They get their name because they have a "rattle" on the end of their tail, made of hard, dead skin, which they shake as a warning when threatened.

A Great Basin rattlesnake, displaying the rattle on the end of its tail.

Black mamba

Living in Africa, this fearsome creature is one of the most venomous snakes in the world. It is also the fastest land snake, slithering along at a speed of up to 12 mph and one of the longest, growing up to 14½ feet.

The black mamba, an extremely dangerous snake from Africa.

The banded sea snake's poison is more powerful than that of any other snake.

Sea snakes

Most snakes live on land, but there is a group of snakes that swim in the sea. The ends of their tails are flattened, like oars, to help them swim. Most sea snakes are very poisonous. Their venom is much stronger than that of most land snakes. They can inflict a deadly bite, especially if they get caught in a fishing net or washed ashore, where someone might tread on them.

MASSIVE MAMMALS

FACT: Hippos and elephants are among the biggest land mammals, and can easily crush a human being with their massive weight.

In Africa, hundreds of people are killed by hippos every year, making it the most dangerous animal on the continent. And many humans think of elephants as friendly animals, but they also regularly attack and kill humans. Grizzly bears are fierce and scary looking, but they are in fact rarely dangerous to humans.

A hippo can weigh as much as 50 men.

Speedy hippo

They look like slow, lumbering beasts that graze peacefully on the grass or float around in rivers. But hippos are big and powerful, have very sharp teeth, and can run surprisingly fast, reaching speeds of up to 25 mph.

Grizzly bears

These are truly massive mammals—a male grizzly bear can weigh over 600 pounds and stand over 7 feet tall on his hind legs. They naturally live in wild, mountainous areas, but in recent years some have been found close to towns after becoming used to humans and their habitats.

A grizzly bear shows off his powerful jaws and teeth.

An elephant can easily overturn a car with its weight and strength.

Elephant charge

Elephants can move fast, too. Just like hippos, they can run 25 mph. So if an elephant charges or attacks, it can be deadly. Female elephants sometimes charge to protect their families, while males can enter a violent state known as **"musth."**

iii

LIONS AND TIGERS

FACT: Big cats—lions and tigers and jaguars and leopards—are the only cats that can roar.

Conservation experts estimate that these amazing animals could be **extinct** by the middle of this century. Incredibly, lions were once the most common large land mammal after humans. They lived in most of Africa, across Europe and America, and in Asia. Today, the few lions and other big cats that still exist live mostly in special **reserves** and protected areas.

A tiger running, showing its distinctive stripes and graceful body.

Big cat

The tiger is the biggest cat in the world. A male can measure up to 12 feet long from nose to tail. That's as long as a car! Tigers are also immensely strong and can cover as much as 30 feet in one leap. Tigers live in India, China, and other parts of Asia, mainly in grassy or forested areas.

COOL!

Pumas can leap an incredible 16 feet high into the air, and up to 33 feet in a long jump.

Lion tale

The lion is famous for being fierce. With his huge mane and terrifying roar, the male lion is known as the "king of the jungle." In fact, lions live in the grasslands of Africa and Asia, not the jungles. They kill fewer people than other wild animals.

Only male lions have the distinctive shaggy mane.

Pumas like to jump on their prey from trees or high rocks.

Leaping puma

The puma—also known as the mountain lion, cougar, or catamount—is a big cat found in North, Central, and South America. Pumas have large, powerful back legs and are brilliant at jumping.

THE DEADLIEST ANIMAL

A mosquito's body fills up with blood as it sucks from its human host.

FACT: Mosquito bites cause around three million deaths around the world each year.

The world's deadliest animal is a tiny insect, a member of the fly family. Mosquitoes suck blood, and when they bite, they spread deadly diseases, including malaria and yellow fever. Although most of these diseases can be treated, mosquitoes often strike in poor areas where people cannot afford medicine or do not have access to health care, so the death toll is very high.

Blood suckers

Mosquitoes don't actually need blood for food. Like butterflies, they feed on fruit and flower nectar. Only the females suck blood, which they need to help them make their eggs.

YIKES!

Diseases spread by mosquitoes are responsible for more human deaths than any other cause, including war, and all other illnesses.

Controlling mosquitoes

Disease-carrying mosquitoes are mainly found in hot, tropical parts of the world, including Africa, southern Asia, and South America. They breed in still water, so swampy places are often breeding grounds. Draining swamps is one way of controlling mosquitoes.

A typical breeding area for mosquitoes.

The mosquito uses its needlelike proboscis to stab through skin and suck up blood.

Needle nose

When it bites, a mosquito jabs the skin with a very long, needlelike mouthpart, called a **proboscis**. This injects an **anticoagulant**—a chemical that stops blood from clotting. Then the mosquito uses its mouth as a straw to suck up the blood.

INSECT STORM

FACT: A single locust swarm can be 460 square miles and can contain 100 billion insects—more locusts than there are people on the planet.

Desert locusts usually lead solitary lives, but sometimes they change to become swarming animals. Many millions of them gather together into a flying **swarm**. The swarm then desends on farmers' fields in a feeding frenzy, devouring crops in minutes. A locust swarm can cause a **famine** by leaving large areas of land with no crops at all.

A swarm of locusts on a beach in Fuerteventura, one of the Canary Islands, Spain.

Solitary to swarm

Desert locusts turn into swarming locusts when a drought follows a heavy rainfall. They breed more during the rainy time, then their food source—plants—dries up in the drought. The brown or green insects become red, yellow, or black and yellow, and begin to swarm together. The swarm then sets off to find new feeding grounds, flying for hundreds of miles.

YIKES!

In the Christian Bible, one of the ten Plagues of Egypt is a plague of locusts, which devours all the crops in Egypt.

Fried locusts wrapped in banana leaves make a tasty treat!

Supper time!

One way of keeping down locust numbers is to eat them up! In Thailand and other Asian countries, grilled locusts are a popular dish. In Nigeria, they are referred to as desert shrimps. Other insects are food for humans too. In fact, in 80 percent of nations people regularly eat insects.

JAWS!

FACT: Sharks never stop growing their razor-sharp teeth, so that when one gets broken a new one takes its place.

There are more than 400 species of sharks in the world's oceans, but only a few of them tear apart their prey with fearsome jaws. If its prey is very large, a shark will clamp down on it and shake its victim to saw off a chunk. There are some scary fish in rivers too.

The sand tiger shark has the sharpest, scariest looking teeth ever!

Tiny teeth

Piranhas are small fish—10 in long—living in the rivers of South America. But they have a set of very sharp teeth, they gather together in **schools**, and they can be aggressive. Piranhas hunt animals, such as birds, that have fallen into the water.

A piranha's bite is powerful enough to snap off a human finger.

COOL!

The biggest sharks, such as basking sharks and whale sharks, are not predators. They swallow tiny sea creatures as they swim along.

A great white shark is photographed from a cage as it attacks tuna bait.

Great white

This monster has the most powerful bite of any shark. Experiments show that just one of its teeth is capable of exerting a force of 132 pounds. With a total biting pressure of many tons this great white could bite through the safety cage if it really wanted to!

DEADLY SEA CREATURES

The box jellyfish hunts crabs and shrimps.

FACT: A sting from a box jellyfish could kill a human in just three minutes.

Some fish and other sea creatures have evolved venomous stings to overcome their prey, or to harm their **predators**. However, some of the venoms affect humans too. They can cause intense pain, **paralysis**, uncontrolled bleeding, and blood poisoning. Sometimes, these symptoms can be fatal.

A sting from the stone fish can be fatal.

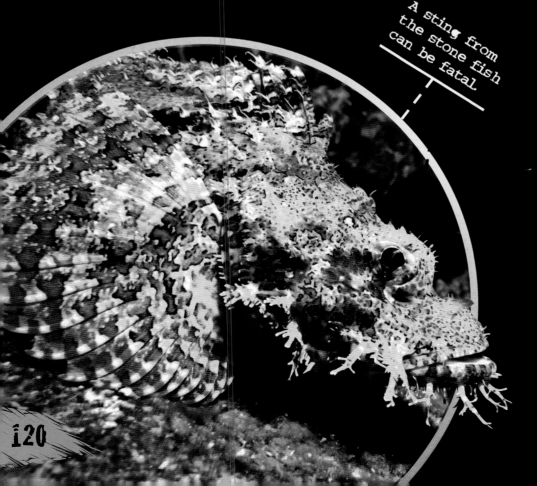

Stone fish

The stone fish lives in the coastal areas of the Indian and Pacific Oceans. Its blotched body resembles a stone, and it may be covered with weeds and anemones to give it extra camouflage. But if a human accidentally steps on it, its spines can pierce the soles of beach shoes to deliver a deadly venom.

When this octopus is provoked, its blue rings become brighter.

These deadly creatures found around Australi in the western Pacifi region, usually in ro or close to the shore blue-ringed octopus tiny—small enough in your hand—yet it a venomus bite capable killing a human. Its poiso works by paralysis, making breathing difficult.

Box jellyfish

The box jellyfish is large, with a cube-shaped top part up to 10 inches across, and stinging tentacles up to 10 feet long. It lives mainly in the Indian and Pacific Oceans. If a swimmer gets caught in its tentacles, the box jellyfish will deliver a sting. This jellyfish's sting is incredibly painful and can cause a

YIKES!

Victims of a sting from a blue-ringed octopus may need a hospital ventilator to help them breathe until the paralysis has passed.

KILLER BEES

FACT: In the 1950s, scientists accidentally created an extra-aggressive breed of bees, known today as killer bees.

The scientists had hoped to make a type of bee that would produce extra honey, but the experiment went wrong. The killer bees reproduced and spread, and can now be found in South and Central America and the southern USA. They do not have a worse sting than ordinary honeybees, but they are more aggressive and more likely to attack in a swarm.

Busy bees, making and maintaining the honeycomb's cells.

Honeybee colony

In a honeybee colony, there are three types of bees: queens, drones, and workers. There is usually a single queen, who lays all the eggs. The job of the drones is to mate with the queen. These bees have no sting. The worker bees do all the hard work in the colony—gathering **pollen** and **nectar**, building the honeycomb cells, and stinging any attackers.

COOL!

The venom from bee stings can be extracted and used to treat athritis and other painful conditions.

122

Bee attack

A single bee sting hurts a little, but is not serious. However, it is really dangerous to be attacked by a whole swarm of bees. This can happen if the bees think their hive is threatened, and killer bees are more likely to perceive a threat than ordinary honeybees. It is difficult to escape such an attack—even jumping in a lake won't help, as the bees will just wait for the person to come up for air.

Worst sting

The tarantula hawk wasp is up to 2 inches long. It has a stinger nearly an inch long, which scares away most predators. For a human, its sting is among the most painful of all insect stings, although thankfully the pain is short-lasting.

A tarantula hawk wasp approaches a tarantula, its typical prey.

YUK!

YIKES!

In the 19th century, diet pills said to contain tapeworm eggs were swallowed up by overweight people in an effort to become slimmer.

FACT: Experts estimate that around a quarter of the world's population is infected with parasitic worms.

Parasitic worms live inside the bodies of their **hosts**, or victims. They feed on the **nutrients** eaten as food by the hosts, causing weight loss and even disease. Most of them lay their eggs outside their host's body.

A tapeworm can grow to 27 feet inside a human intestine.

Cyst to tapeworm

A tapeworm **larva** is called a cyst. Cysts are sometimes found in dirty water or undercooked meat. Once ingested, the cyst grows into an adult tapeworm inside the body's intestines. As its name suggests, it is tape-shaped, with little hooks on its head to fix itself firmly to the inside of the intestine.

Threadworm life cycle

People catch threadworms by swallowing their eggs in dirty water, food, or on their hands. The eggs hatch into worms that live in the intestines. Female worms lay eggs around the anus, making it itchy. Scratching gets the eggs into fingernails which may then later go into mouths, causing more infection. Luckily threadworms are easily treated with medication.

Guinea worm

This evil parasite affects humans and other animals in Africa and Asia. The larvae of the worm live in stagant water, so infect people who don't have a clean water supply. Inside the body, a female worm continues growing until it is ready to lay eggs. Then, it emerges from the body, making a nasty blister.

125

BODY BUGS

FACT: Head lice cannot fly, swim or jump, so they rely on head-to-head contact between people to form new colonies.

Head lice are just one of the tiny bugs that feed entirely on blood—of humans and other animals. Head lice live on our bodies all their lives. Other body bugs hitch a ride, suck the blood they need, then move on to another victim.

Bed bugs live in people's beds, biting them when they are asleep.

Night feeder

At night-time, bed bugs jab their sleeping victims with sharp, beaklike mouthparts that have two tubes in them—one for injecting painkilling chemicals, the other for sucking blood. Bed bugs hate light, so they disappear during the day. They are small and flat and can hide in mattress seams and tiny cracks.

YIKES!

Ticks may carry several diseases, including Lyme disease, which can cause damage to the nervous system if untreated.

Home is where the head is

On a human head, the female louse lays eggs close to a hair root, using a special glue to stick it to the hair. As soon as the larva hatches, it starts to bite the head and suck up the blood. Each louse lives for about four weeks, sucking blood and laying eggs.

Head louse eggs, or nits, glued to human hair.

This tick is growing fat and swollen as it fills with human blood.

Filling station

Ticks don't stay on their hosts all the time. They live in long grass or on trees, and brush onto people or other animals' bodies as they go past. The tick finds some bare skin and burrows its sharp mouthparts, and most of its head, into the flesh. It can hang on for minutes, hours, or even days as it drinks its fill of tasty blood.

HOUSEHOLD BUGS

FACT: Cockroaches are probably the world's hardiest bugs, able to survive without food for a month, and without air for 45 minutes.

Cockroaches are also very hard to catch or kill, as they can flatten their bodies into tiny cracks and crevices. No wonder they are an unwelcome visitor in our homes! Even if a home is cockroach-free, it is likely to be inhabited by other disease-spreading household bugs. Some of them are so small they can't even be seen.

Disease spreaders

Some cockroaches have adapted to life in human homes. They live in kitchens and bathrooms, coming out at night to feed on leftover food and garbage. Many people are revolted by cockroaches, which can spread dangerous disease germs. Yuck!

Cockroaches feast on a half-eaten sandwich.

Fly feast

Houseflies have spongelike mouths that can only soak up liquid food. So, after landing on a piece of cake, a housefly spits and vomits onto it, to make the food mushy and break it down into liquid. When it's nice and runny, the fly sucks up as much as it can, leaving some spit and vomit behind. While feeding, flies also poo constantly, so they leave that behind, too!

YIKES!

Houseflies lay their eggs in rubbish or animal poo, which the developing maggots then feed on.

Buzzing, slurping houseflies feast on ham that has been left uncovered.

Munch, munch

Teeny tiny dust mites live in most homes, and feed on people's dead skin flakes. As they munch their way through dust and skin bits, they leave droppings, as well as their own skins, which they shed like a snake does. These substances can cause serious **allergies** in some people, giving them asthma or a rash.

A microscopic view of a dust mite, a big fan of dead skin for dinner.

DUNG BEETLES

FACT: Dung beetles help to tidy up the landscape, discourage pests, recycle nutrients, and improve the soil.

Some beetles have developed odd habits and peculiar ways to fight off predators or feed their young. The bombardier beetle can shoot out an explosive mixture of hot, revolting-smelling liquid and gas. Some beetles use their own poo as a protective material, and others feed on dung—the poo of **herbivorous** animals.

Mmm, dinner! Dung beetles zero in on a fresh pile of dung.

A dung life

Some dung beetles live in piles of dung, but most shape it into neat balls, roll it away, and bury it in the ground to keep it safe. Then they lay eggs inside the dung ball and guard the babies as they grow inside it. When they hatch out, the babies feed on the dung.

COOL!

For the ancient Egyptians, the dung beetle represented the sun god Ra, who was said to roll the sun across the sky each day.

Deadly spray

The bombardier beetle's body contains two chemicals. When danger threatens, the chemicals combine to make heat and gas, and pressure shoots the gas out of the beetle's behind. This ferocious spurt of chemicals can seriously injure or even kill predators such as spiders, frogs, and other beetles.

A bombardier can swivel its tail end around to aim its weapon anywhere.

This tiny but stinky pile of poo is actually a tortoise beetle larva, hiding beneath its protective poo shield.

Poo armor

Several species of beetle have a strange habit—they cover their eggs in a thick coating of poo! This hardens into a solid shell that protects the young from predators. When the beetle hatches, it adds to the shell with its own poo, forming a kind of armor plating, which scientsts call a fecal shield.

CREEPY CRAWLIES

FACT: Worldwide, there are 10,000 species of millipede and 8,000 species of centipede.

Millipedes are the ultimate creepy crawlies. They have more legs than any other animal on Earth—one species was found to have 750! In spite of their creepy appearance, millipedes are mostly harmless. This is not the case for their cousins, the centipedes. These creepies generally have fewer legs, but they are carnivorous and venomous.

Monster millipede

Most millipedes are only a few inches long. But the giant African millipede is a monster that can grow to be over 12 inches long and is as thick as your thumb. Like earthworms, millipedes don't hunt or eat other animals. They burrow through soil and rotting plants, munching as they go.

Imagine how this enormous millipede must tickle!

COOL!

Millipedes' multiple legs move rather slowly, in a wave-like pattern. Centipedes can scuttle along much faster.

Peruvian centipede

These beasties are agggressive predators, hunting anything they can find, including mice and birds. Their venom is poisonous to humans too—a bite will cause severe pain and fever. These centipedes are big as well as nasty—they can be up to 12 inches long.

The Peruvian giant yellow-legged centipede.

Tiger centipede

The Mediterranean tiger centipede can be found throughout southern Spain and North Africa. When attacking, the tiger centipede uses its whole body to fiercely grip its prey. It sometimes lives in people's homes, hiding during the day and roaming about at night. Its bite is very painful to a human.

The Mediterranean tiger centipede has a striped yellow and black body.

BRINGING UP BABIES

FACT: The female Surinam toad nurtures its young on its back, popping them out when they are fully grown.

The Surinam toad, despite its name, is actually a frog found in rivers and ponds in South America. It has one of the most amazing ways of giving birth!

A mother Surinam toad with her back covered in pockets of skin, containing growing baby frogs.

Growing up

After the female toad has laid her eggs, the male collects them and presses them onto her back. Skin grows over to protect them. In little pockets under the female's skin, the eggs hatch and grow. After several months, the baby frogs shoot out and swim free. Each baby is around 1 inch long.

Child care spider style

Wolf spiders are the most protective mothers in the spider family. After laying eggs, the female carries the **egg sac** around, holding it carefully so it doesn't get damaged. When the eggs hatch out, the tiny spiderlings clamber on to their mother's back and she continues to care for them.

A wolf spider with all her spiderlings on her back.

ANIMAL HEALING

FACT: A nasty, gangrenous wound that's failing to heal could be treated with an application of live, wriggling, hungry maggots.

But if a doctor doesn't decide on maggots to clean up a wound, bloodthirsty leeches may be applied. Leeches, like maggots, are increasingly being used in medicine. Even ants can be put to a medicinal use.

Medical maggots

These medical maggots are specially bred and free of germs. They eat up the dead tissue, so they will naturally keep a wound clean. To make sure they can breathe and move around, doctors apply them to the wound inside a loose dressing with airholes in it. They can stay in there for days!

A doctor applies a special maggot-filled dressing to a wound

What's it used for?

Because leeches suck blood, they can be used to vacuum up clogged or infected blood from wounds, leaving them cleaned and healthy. Another useful job they can do is suck blood into body parts that have been re-attached—for example, fingers that have been chopped off and sewn back on. The leech is placed on the re-attached part, and as it sucks it increases blood flow where the parts have been surgically joined.

A doctor carefully applies a leech to skin after surgery.

A safari ant in action.

Ant stitches

Although the soldier safari ant's bite is painful, it's very useful for closing up gashes and injuries, in the same way that stitches and sutures are used in hospitals. Pulling the cut closed, then holding a soldier ant up to the wound will make the ant bite the edges together. Then, the rest of the ant's body can be snapped off, leaving the jaws in place. They can stay there for up to a week.

137

SURPRISING SUPPERS

FACT: Many African and Asian people consider cheese to be disgusting.

We all eat foods that people from different cultures find revolting! All over southern Africa, cheese might be frowned upon but a type of caterpillar is a staple food. In Australia, witchetty grubs have been a traditional snack for thousands of years. In some Scandinavian countries the Christmas speciality is not roast turkey or plum pudding but ... sheep's head!

These witchetty grubs are being prepared for cooking.

Moth larvae

"Grub" is another name for a larva, or baby insect. Witchetty grubs are a type of moth larvae, so they are really a kind of caterpillar. The larvae can grow to 2.8 inches long, and are eaten raw, fried, and roasted.

Caterpillar season

Mopane worms aren't actually worms, but a type of moth caterpillar. They hatch in early summer and crawl all over mopane trees, feeding and growing fat. People gather them, then dry them in the sun. They are also canned and sold in supermarkets. In fact, mopane worms are such an important food that during worm season, sales of other meat drop dramatically.

Mopane worms are being cooked over an open fire here, ready for a feast.

A cooked sheep's head, served with sausage.

Sheep's head

To prepare a sheep's head, it is first washed well, and the hair scraped off. Then it is salted and soaked in water. The head is then boiled for several hours with chopped vegetables, or roasted in an oven. It is often served with potatoes or crusty bread and a tomato sauce.

139

GLOSSARY

Acrophobia
a terror of heights. Most people have some fear of heights.

Allergies
extreme reactions to things that are harmless or mildly harmful to most humans. Some people are allergic to bee and wasp stings, making a sting very dangerous for them.

Anticoagulant
a substance that prevents the blood clotting. Blood-sucking insects often inject an anticoagulant into their victims.

Atmosphere
Earth's atmosphere is a layer of gases that surround our planet and make life on it possible.

Aurora borealis
bands of colored light that appear in the night sky. Commonly called the northern lights.

Bacteria
microscopic, single-celled creatures that are neither plants nor animals. They were probably the first life-forms to exist on Earth.

Calligrapher
a calligrapher is an expert in producing beautiful, decorative lettering, or handwriting.

Carrion
the carcass, or body, of a dead animal.

Catacombs
human-made caves originally built for religious ceremonies.

Causeways
a causeway is a load or railway that crosses a large body of water, such as a lake.

Crevasse
a deep crack in a glacier or an ice sheet. A crack in rock is called a crevice.

Dunes
a dune is a hill made of sand, in the desert created by wind and on the coast by water.

Dust devil
a spinning column of wind, dust, and debris. Dust devils occur in dry, sandy places.

Ecosystem
a community of animals and plants sharing an environment with non-living things such as water, soil, or climate, so that both animals and environment benefit from the relationship.

Egg sac
a silky pouch in which spiders deposit their eggs.

Electrical charge
A build-up of electricity, either positively or negatively charged.

Electromagnets
magnets in which the magnetic field is controlled by the flow of electricity. When the electricity is stopped the magnetic field disappears.

Electrons
an electron is a particle that carries a single negative electrical charge.

Elliptical orbit
oval, rather than circular, orbit. This happens because the orbiting object increases in speed when it enters the gravity field of the planet or other body it is orbiting.

Extinct
when all the members of an animal species, or examples of a plant species, have died out it has become extinct.

Famine
A severe shortage of food resulting in starvation.

Fault line
a place where two of Earth's tectonic plates meet, often the site of frequent earthquakes.

Glacier
a massive block of ice that is moving very slowly.

Gorge
a steep valley between two cliffs, usually created by the flow of a river over millions of years.

Haboob
an intense duststorm that particularly affects Sudan in Africa, but may occur in any desert.

Herbivorous
animals that are herbivorous eat only plants.

Hosts
Parasitic animals, often tiny creatures, live on hosts—larger animals. They often take their nourishment from food the host eats.

Hotspots
areas in the middle of a tectonic plate, where magma from inside Earth rises up to create a volcano.

Hydrothermal vent site
deep under the sea, an area of chimney-like structures that spew out mineral-rich hot water, which supports various life-forms.

Iceberg
a chunk of ice that has broken off from a glacier. Icebergs are much larger below sea level.

Interstellar space
also called outer space, interstellar space is beyond our solar system.

Larva
a larva is a wormlike baby of an animal such as a butterfly.

Lava
magma that has erupted onto the surface from a volcano.

Liquifies
turning to liquid. Spiders liquify their prey's insides with chemicals.

Livestock
animals that are farmed by humans such as sheep, pigs, and cows.

Low pressure
when the atmospheric pressure of an air mass is lower than its surroundings it can be said to have low pressure.

Magma
molten, or hot liquified rock below Earth's surface.

Magnetic field
an area stretching from Earth's core out into space, where objects are influenced by magnetic forces.

Migration
the regular journey of animals from one place to another, and then back again, usually for food or climate.

Minerals
a mineral is a natural solid made of a particular mix of chemicals. Some minerals are nutritional to humans and other creatures.

Moai
huge rock statues probably depicting ancestors on Easter Island, Polynesia.

Molecules
a molecule is a group of atoms that stick together. Molecules are too small to see without a powerful microscope. They can be dust in space.

Mopane
the mopane tree grows in Africa. Its leaves are eaten by the mopane caterpillar.

Mummies
a mummy is a body that has been preserved by chemicals, either accidentally or deliberately.

Musth
an aggressive state that affects male elephants regularly. They may attack humans when in musth.

Nectar
a sweet liquid produced by plants to attract pollinating insects such as bees.

Nutrients
chemicals that plants or animals need for good health.

Ossuary
a place where human skeletons are stored. Ossuaries are used mostly when there is a shortage of burial space.

Paralysis
when a person is paralyzed they cannot move part of or their whole body. Some venomous animals paralyze their victims.

Pollen
a powder produced by plants to reproduce, and collected by bees for food.

Predators
a predator is an animal that hunts another animal—its prey.

Proboscis
a long nose-like body part on an animal's head. In insects, it is used as a sucking mouth.

Polyp
a tiny coral creature.

Pyroclastic flow
a burning cloud of gas, dust, ash, and rocks, that may flow down a mountain after a volcanic eruption.

Rabies
a deadly disease that humans can contract from animal bites.

Reserves
an animal reserve is a place where wild animals can live, protected from human hunters.

GLOSSARY

Reservoir
a human-made lake for storing water. Reservoirs are usually created in river valleys by building a dam.

Satellite
a natural or human-made object that revolves around a planet in orbit.

Schools
a school of fish is a group that swims together.

Spacewalk
an astronaut moving around in space outside the spacecraft is on a space walk. May also be called extra vehicular activity (EVA).

Space probe
an unmanned craft sent to explore space.

Solar system
our sun and all the planets that travel around it, including Earth.

Stalactites
a deposit of minerals that hangs from the ceilings and walls of limestone caves. Deposits that grow upward from the cave floor are called stalagmites.

Swarm
A large number of insects flying together.

Tectonic plates
the slabs of solid rock that fit together like jigsaw pieces to make up Earth's surface. Most volcanoes and earthquakes occur where the plates meet.

Trawler
a boat used for commercial fishing.

Time zones
areas, usually countries, keep to the same time and are in one time zone. Crossing time zones means moving from an area with one time zone to an area with a different one.

Vapor
water vapor is the gas form of water. It forms when water reaches boiling point, called steam, or as water slowly evaporates.

Venom
the toxins that some animals inject into their prey, to cause pain or death.

Vertical
straight up or down.

Volcanologist
a scientist who studies volcanoes.

Vortex
a mass of spinning air, liquid or dust, which forms a hole at its center.

Waterspout
a spinning column of water created by a whirlwind, that occurs over a body of water by a whirlwind.

Whirlpool
a powerful current of water, flowing in a downward spiral. Whirlpools are caused by two tides flowing in opposite directions.

INDEX